First published in 2006
by WOW Worldwide Ltd.
All rights reserved.
Text and illustrations copyright © 2006 WOW Worldwide Ltd

A CIP Catalogue record for this book is available on request.

ISBN 10: 0-9547283-4-3
ISBN 13: 978-0-9547283-4-2

Series editor:
Kathy Robinson
Kathy Robinson is the founder of the "Signs for Success" programme which uses sign language to raise levels of reading, writing and spelling in young hearing children.

Series sign consultant:
Frances Elton - City University, London

Character Design/Art Direction:
Sam Williams

Illustration:
Andrew Crowson

Design:
Scott Gibson

Printed in China

WOW uses British Sign Language (BSL).

Fingerspelling
Alphabet

WOW Worldwide

Get the most from your **WOW Kids** Fingerspelling Alphabet book.

Fingerspell with me now!
It's fun, it's easy,
and I'll show you how!

- Point to the letter.
- Make the sound of the letter as you fingerspell it.
- Say the letter again.
- Do this for each letter, and then you can try fingerspelling simple words, such as "cat", "dog" and "hat".

 **Have fun!**

Aa

Bb

Cc

Dd

Ee

Ff

G g

Hh

Ii

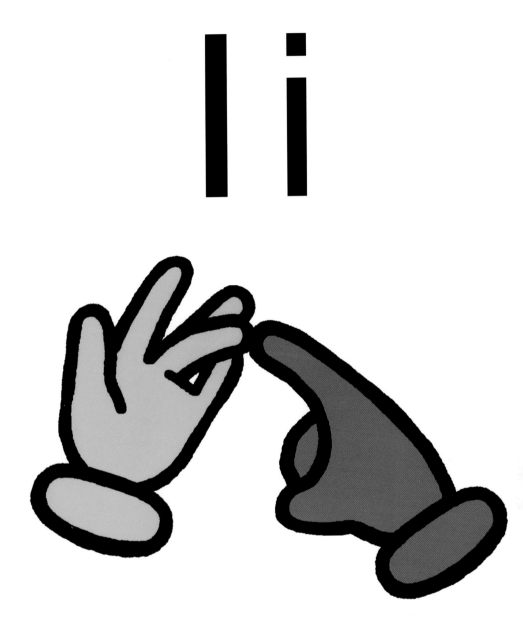

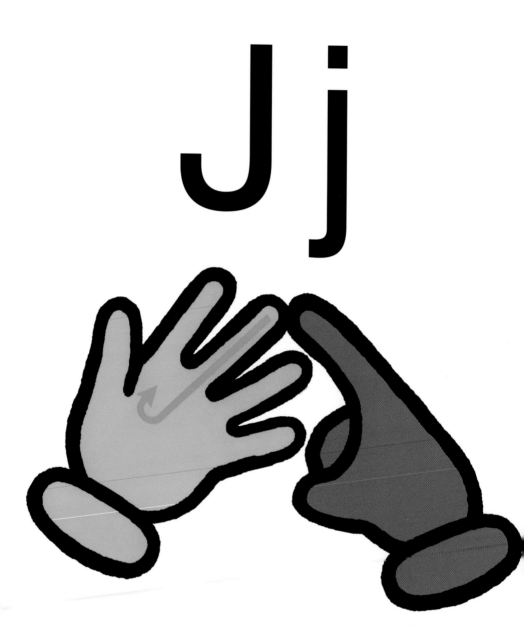

Kk

L l

M m

Nn

Oo

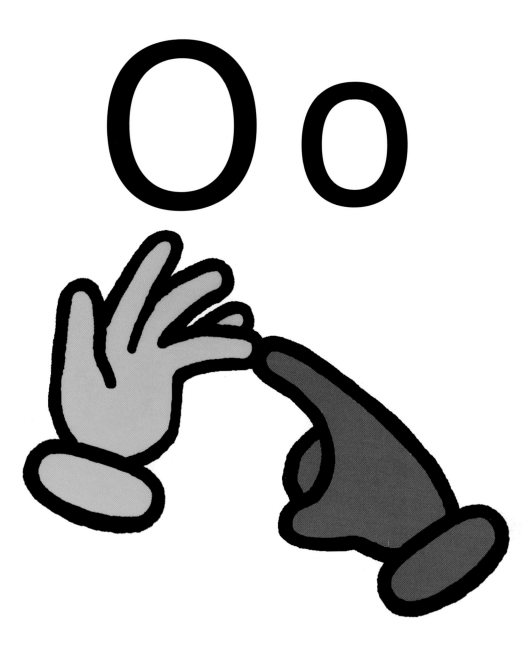

Pp

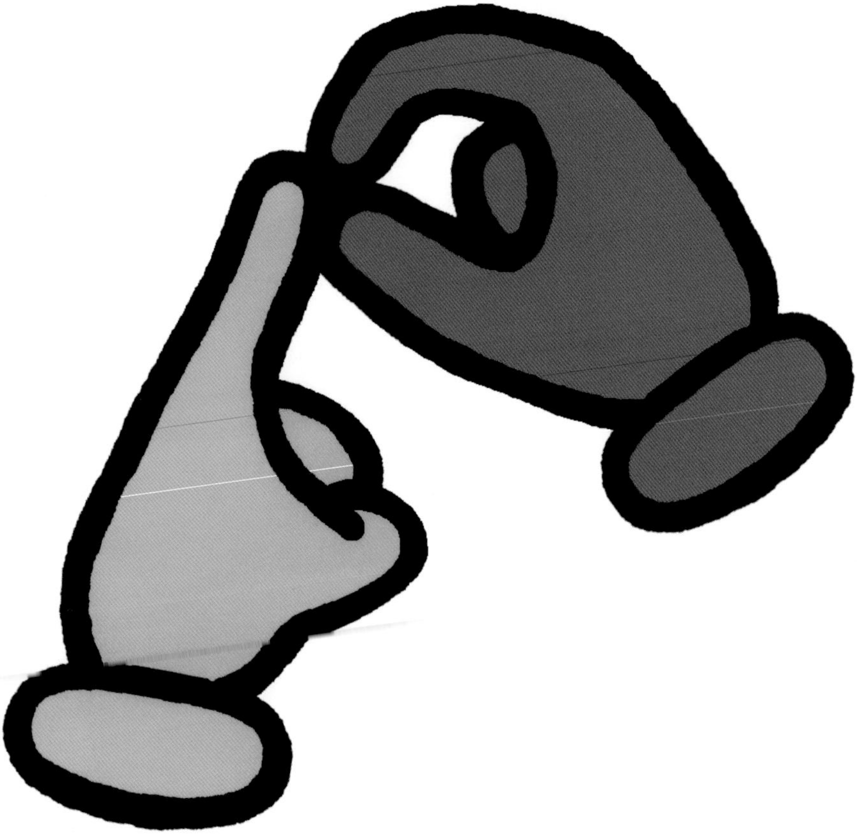

Q q

Rr

S s

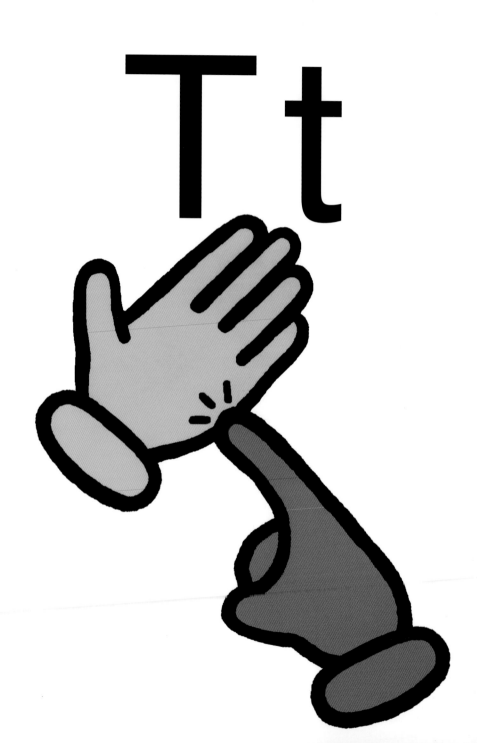

Vv

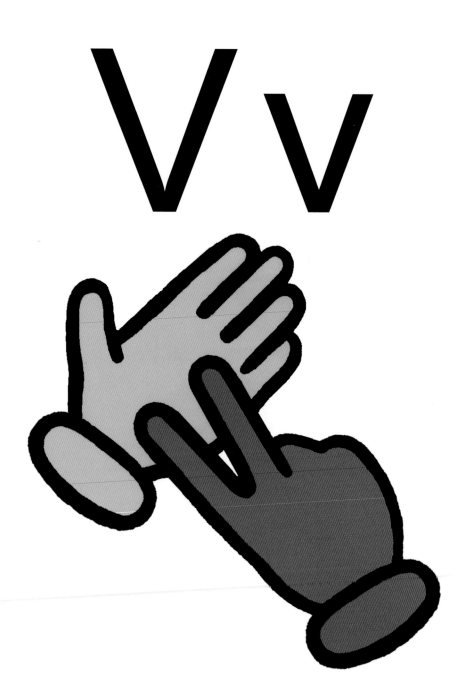

Ww

Xx

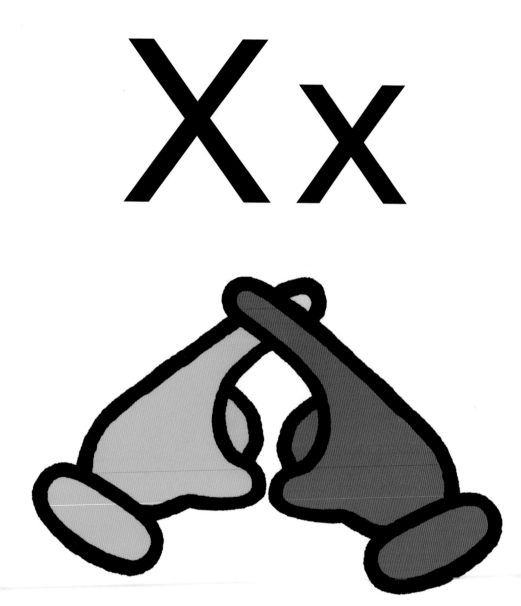

Yy

Zz

WOW™

You're so clever!

For more fingerspelling fun and useful information go to www.wowworldwide.co.uk